The People
&
The Land

By

Champion Muthle

DEDICATION

For my grandparents.
For all those whose land and inheritance have been
stolen. For Cullinan and our diamonds.

ACKNOWLEDGMENTS

Rodó, Paz, Neruda, Borges and Martí.
Mis Padrinos.

"This land is your land, this land is my land
From California to the New York Island
From the Redwood Forest to the Gulf Stream waters
This land was made for you and me."

- Woody Guthrie, *This Land Is Your Land* (1944)

What is our relationship to the land?

Are we not its rightful owners and heirs?

Is it not José Martí who rides at the entrance of that Great Park?

Is it not César Chávez and Che Guevarra whose images adorn the walls and murals of our great cities?

Yet the Oligarchs would have us believe that we are mere gardeners and *illegals*.

How can one be a vagrant in his own garden?
An intruder on his own shores?

No one is *illegal.*

Was Jesus not also portrayed as a simple gardener?

The wind and the rain have no claim to the ground under our feet, other than what they help cultivate.

So too have the seeds of Colonialism fallen upon us, not us upon them.

And what has Colonialism cultivated other than poverty, division, and malnutrition?

We cannot eat the wind.
We cannot eat the rain.
But with them we can cultivate the future.

The land is indispensable.

As I walk through the Hawaiian Islands, I learn nothing new from the White man about compost other than how to enrich his desire for authority and recognition.

Like shit, I fertilize his desire.

I follow the runoff downstream, to the colonial Sugar
Mill, that has poisoned the beach.

There are no more fish in this pond.
There is no more food to eat.

And somehow I am the one to blame at dinner time.

My bait is not made of magic.
My rod is not a wand.

What few incantations I do know, I would use to cleanse the shores of your cruelty and excrement.

Now bite this ghost pepper and cleanse your soul.

I do not wish to form burdensome ties to the past, as we emerge from its maze.

Humanity can only survive so much suffering and torture.

Let us not delay our departure.

Let us not cause undue pain.

26

Let not our memory be an impediment to our future.

I have searched and walked the maze far and wide.
I have mapped its each and every turn.

There are no hidden treasures under its bushels.
There are no answers to its riddles.

The fruit it does bear, hangs from the top of the tallest tree, where we can still yet breathe the air of a new and fresh atmosphere.

But we should not be forced to make a daily climb just to enjoy the riches of the Tree of Life.

We are not Monkeys.
We are not Apes.
We are not Baboons.

We are the people of the land.
And the land is for us.

Let us not speak romantically about our wanderings.

Let us speak practically and true.

The land is not just land.

The land is development, dignity, stability and culture.

The land is Earth, Ocean, Sky, and Space.

The land is dwelling, dreamscape, food and final resting place.

As Neruda writes, En Ti La Tierra.

Do we not dream in equal measure?

Are we not, rich and poor, equal owners of the future?

42

From the closest shores to the farthest stars, do our hearts and eyes not cover the same distance?

Despite who gets there first, are we not all part of the same journey?

It is not enough to empower the poor or penalize the rich.

We must chart a new course.
One that brings us both closer to each other, closer to our dreams, and closer to the land itself.

Our destiny awaits us there, at the end of the rainbow, at the bottom of the waterfall, in the deepest, darkest cave from which we all came…

...And to which we will all return someday.

ABOUT THE AUTHOR

Champion Muthle aka Daniel Maree is an award-winning Writer-Director, Creative and Cultural Strategist, Independent Journalist, Inventor, Philosopher, Creative Technologist, Afro-Futurist, and Social Entrepreneur. He is a Frederick Douglass Scholar and Forbes 30 Under 30 Honoree for Social Entrepreneurship. His work has been featured in the MoMA and the Library of Congress.

www.ingramcontent.com/pod-product-compliance
Lightning Source LLC
Chambersburg PA
CBHW051418250726
48655CB00003B/1108